Eat at the Table

Your Life Made to Order

TALISHA L. BENNETT, MBA

Copyrighted Material

EAT AT THE TABLE

Copyright © 2015 by TLB Bookkeeping Services. ALL RIGHTS RESERVED

No part of this publication may be reproduced, stored in a retrieval system or transmitted, in any form or by any means—electronic, mechanical, photocopying, recording or otherwise—without prior written permission from the publisher, except for the inclusion of brief quotations in a review.

For information about this title or to order other books and/or electronic media, contact the publisher:

TLB Bookkeeping Services
P.O. Box 962625
El Paso TX 79996
www.tlbbookkeeping.com
publishing@tlbbookkeeping.com

Library of Congress Control Number: 2014915086

ISBN: 978-0-9907195-0-2

ISBN: 978-0-9907195-1-9 (eBook)

Printed in the United States of America

Cover and Interior design: 1106 Design, *www.1106design.com*

Book Dedication

I dedicate this book to my father and
mother, Samuel and Betty Fisher.
I've always hoped to make you both proud.

Daddy, as always, your presence was what
I needed in my life. Thanks for keeping
me laughing and allowing me to spend
time with you. Your silent and soft-spoken
disposition spoke volumes to me.

Mom, thank you for always speaking
encouraging words to create positive change
in my life. Your words and stories are
priceless. You, my dear, are a book
to be read, a voice to be heard,
and a woman to be valued.

You both have been through a lot,
and you've sacrificed a lot; may the joy
of your years be restored so greatly,
none would seem lost.

A single conversation across the table with a wise man is better than ten years mere study of books.

Henry Wadsworth Longfellow

Table of Contents

CHAPTER 1
Eat at the Table   1

CHAPTER 2
Memories and a Meal   7

CHAPTER 3
Words Matter   19

CHAPTER 4
Who's Feeding You?   33

CHAPTER 5
Pounding Crumbs into Bread   45

CHAPTER 6
Prepared to Be Served   53

CHAPTER 7
Life Made to Order   65

Call Outs and Quotes   73

About the Author   79

Preface

In our present, fast-paced, "I want everything right now" culture, we are being systematically stripped of the traditional family values that serve as the foundation upon which societies safely rest. Our hectic, on-the-go lifestyles are robbing our children of those vital, moral, and ethical nutrients that have fed humankind since the dawn of civilization. Consequently, families are no longer equipped with the tools necessary to send their children into the world: a proper understanding of the values needed to succeed in life and the quality of life to which people should aspire, and a commitment to preserve important family bonds and traditions.

Our world seems to be operating according to a much faster clock than the one our parents enjoyed, leaving the current generation struggling to keep up. One of the main culprits dissolving the family structure is our society's unhealthy obsession with convenience.

While modern conveniences are precious time savers, there is a downside to every technological improvement that finds its way into our lifestyles; it seems that every convenience somehow displaces one of our time-honored traditions. In our pursuit of convenience, stopping long enough to spend quality time with precious family members has become an inconvenient burden that many people cannot endure. We have become too busy to simply sit down, live in the moment, and cast all cares and anxieties aside. We are left too busy to relax and too divided to come together. And, in the wake of our convenient lifestyles, we have been zapped of the optimism that causes us to see brighter tomorrows, dream bigger dreams, and map out our futures.

There is a place, however, to which we can all return—a place crucial to humankind's narrative since the very beginning of time. I am speaking of a place we all have the means of obtaining, a place that welcomes us with open arms and receives us just as we are. It is a retreat and a safe haven that does not hold time against us. It patiently waits for our arrival and quietly keeps us company, whether or not we recognize the valuable role it plays in our lives. It is as small or as large as we want or need it to be. This is a very common place, one that transcends cultures and generations. This one place has many purposes, yet it provides something essential to all who meet there. This place is "The Table."

I believe there is one simple yet values-instilling tradition every family should embrace: eating at the table. Those who once had this tradition should revisit it. Family mealtime is more than the act of sitting in the same location merely to consume food. When family members come together at the dinner table, much more is digested than food. By default, the dinner table serves as the one place where parents pass along important values to their children, and where children communicate their fears, hurts, and concerns to their parents. This tradition holds more than just the idea of family time and supper; it is neutral ground to all and a place of feeding on lessons to be learned and experiences to be addressed and used as teaching moments.

Time at the table should be focused and purposeful. Considering the many changes in society, as well as changes in the social norms of the culture, the table is one place where the entire family can come together and be refreshed, restored, redirected, and real. No longer should eating on the go be the norm for your family. The act of sitting is one that says, "My time is now yours and you are worth it." Through this simple gesture, the recipient may feel a sense of being wanted or needed, and, most importantly, family members should feel that what they received at the table—in addition to the food—was worthy of their investment of time. More than just a physical table where food is consumed, we must consider that our lives are a table that family and friends come to, where our very words are the food that is consumed.

While food is important (and some people even go to cooking classes to learn to cook), the words and wisdom that are imparted are even more important and are absorbed by those around the table more often than we think—yet we don't go to cooking classes to learn how to "cook our words."

This book will show you ways to include meeting at the table in your busy schedule, and show you the benefits to yourself and your family of doing so. You can also consider this book to be a "word cookbook," showing you how to season and simmer your words so you can prepare them just as carefully as you would a meal. And hopefully you will find a moment to come to grips with your own past, whether good or bad, so that in "coming to the table" you are able to give of yourself freely in hopes that someone's life will be impacted as your life was, or as you would have hoped it could have been.

Consider the possibilities—the lessons that can be learned, the stories that can be shared, the lives that can be changed—when time is not an issue. No clocks, no phones, no Internet, no rushing, and no interruptions. Eat at the table and correct your past, establish your future, and live in the moment, while you have it. Please accept my invitation to Come, Sit, and Eat!

Acknowledgments

To my husband Charles, "I love you to life." Thanks for being a great friend and an amazing father. And thank you for allowing me the time needed to complete this book.

A special thanks to my crew, also known as the Little Bennetts. I want you all to make us proud and live your dreams. I love you all dearly.

Adria, stay creative and complete whatever you set out to do. Your work is greater than you give yourself credit for. Be okay with you. You're amazing.

Charles IV, my Olympian. You are an absolute jewel to me, son. Live your dreams. You are already a Champion and the essence of hard work and dedication.

Cyesha, my affectionate one. Continue standing tall and being strong. Keep at your music and keep your heart open to God. You have already written songs that inspire me; now inspire the world.

To my baby girl, Cya—the educator. Stay bold and sure of who you are. Stay on the path that has been laid for you.

To my siblings, you all were so fun to live with.

Kwemana (Manny)—the genius and the essence of what a big brother should be. I always felt safe and cared for by you.

Amina, you are a testimony to be told and a story to be written. You are my favorite big sister ever....

Samuel (Keedie), I love you to pieces. I am grateful for the years shared together in high school. You will always be my favorite football player.

Kendrick (we will meet again).

My twin, DeShone, the cutest and coolest guy I know. I thank God He chose you to be a part of my life.

And finally to my little brother, the baby of the bunch, the funniest young man to have grown up with—Dennis (Disco). I love you and pray you never lose your sense of humor and that huge smile.

A very special thanks to someone who made it okay for me to be me. She is a major part of my life and by way of my nephew and niece, she will forever be a part of it—Serena (Renie Mac). You are a sister to me and a forever friend. We have some great stories together. I crack up just thinking about the foolishness we did. Lord help us!

To my host of nephews and nieces, I pray you know just how amazing your parents are and how much you should value them and your grandparents. Love Tia!!!! MAKE ME PROUD. You are all added blessings to me whether you know it or not. I love you all.

To my parents who have continued in raising me, Dr. Mikel and Mother Debra Brown. Sir, thank you for pouring into my life—even during the time of my reluctance. I still say that you are the best thing to happen to my marriage. There is so much to be said, I cannot begin to put it into words. Thank you is not enough. Mother, thank you for being consistent in who you are as a mom, a person, and a First Lady. Thanks for showing me how to be strong as a woman, balanced as a mom, submissive in ministry, and supportive as a wife. You give more than we could ever imagine. I value you.

To my Uncle Alfred Jordan, (SURPRISE) you would never know just how much of a blessing you were to my life at the very moment I needed it most.

A major thanks to DelGar Publishing, Gary Sparkman (author of *Dare to Discover Yourself*), and my dear sisters Delores Sparkman and Caryn Newman. Thank you for your professional help with the book: your eyes, your honesty, and encouraging words.

To my Christian Joy Center family and friends: Thanks for being family to me and my kids, especially Grandma Nell.

To every person who has ever been a part of my life; for every trial and victory, THANK YOU! I hold no regrets. You've added to my journey.

I've grown and I've survived.

Chapter 1
Eat at the Table

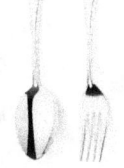

Lost time is never found again.
Benjamin Franklin

I have heard stories of—and have personally experienced—families and friends coming together for special occasions, or for no apparent occasion at all; they would gather for no particular reason or season. One way or another, they came together, only to find themselves meeting at the table. The table becomes a common ground that minimizes all differences while exposing them at the same time.

The table puts all who meet at it in a non-threatening position and there is no need for self-defense. The table is the one place where people willingly meet, where no one expects an invitation to approach. The table holds the thrilling potential for so many positive things: eating, talking, laughing, praying, disagreeing, and even experiencing awkward moments of silence.

> *The table becomes a common ground that minimizes all differences while exposing them at the same time.*

The act of sitting at the table creates an atmosphere for hearing new stories and retelling old stories, again and again. At the table, we learn of a person's past, and we get a glimpse into a person's future. With their words, they paint a picture of their futures on the canvases of our minds, all while giving hope to eager listeners about their own lives. We continue in conversation and willingly endure those moments again and again (because they are precious moments), and although at times we may seem quiet and awkward, conversation ensues.

Around the table we discuss new topics, view new faces, and hear the many voices of those at the table or chiming in from another room, throwing in their two cents worth. The table makes it okay for each participant to let down his or her usual defenses, as each person senses there will be no indictment for ideas expressed. Without hesitation or reluctance, without knowing the outcome or possibilities, and without regard for any negative outcomes, we willingly show up to the table to face it all again. What eating at the table draws from us and instills in us makes every visit worthwhile, and gives us every reason to replay the moments all over again.

Numerous studies underscore the many positive outcomes of families coming together around family meals, and show conclusive evidence of the many positive effects of eating together as a family. These positive effects range from weight control, to the development of positive social skills, to openness with family members and friends.

Most of the studies I have read speak mainly of the positive benefits for children. One article in particular, titled "Benefits of the Dinner Table Ritual" was published in a May 2005 edition of the *New York Times*. The article makes note of the difference between children and teenagers who experience some table time with their family during the week versus those who do not. According to the article, this one activity—a simple family meal—can determine the type of friends most children will have. The article goes on to cite studies done by the Archives of Pediatrics and Adolescent Medicine, and the National Center on Addiction and Substance Abuse at Columbia University. It is interesting to note that these studies correlate a significant decrease in the amount of family time at the dinner table with a tremendous demand for cookbooks and guides for quick ways to feed a family. These studies also attribute the rise in fast food consumption to a lack of time spent at the table. Even with the option of quick meals and food on the go, quality time together still goes lacking.

What seems to make the table—whether that table is at home or at a restaurant—so unique is what happens there. Through many conversations and observations, I have found that the table is the place where joy, fear, laughter, anxiety, and real feelings cannot hide. The table is where teaching happens and instructions are given. Furthermore, the table is where our children cannot ignore the important values we

> *The table must be preserved as the one place where the official, unwritten rule must be: Listen to me and hear me out.*

choose to instill in them. At the table, children can neither run nor hide from the critical data parents should be downloading into their open minds. The table must be preserved as the one place where the official, unwritten rule must be: Listen to me and hear me out.

How do we come to this place with such an openness and willingness to gather? How do we come to this place where the things said or done are forgiven and resolved the moment they occur? Why such comfort for many, and why such discomfort for some—yet they find themselves at the table anyway? What draws us to that place, besides our need for food, a quiet place to read, or simply to be alone? Moreover, why is gathering together at the table such a rare event for too many families?

I find it fascinating that more eating is done than we realize, whether it was in my childhood home or in my current household; we consume more than food. Though the desire to eat may be the main reason to come to the table, if we are open when we arrive at the table, we will depart having consumed more than we expected. Yes, the food is there, but so too are the memories created, the history exposed, and the legacies established that propel us into our futures. We are there consuming conversations and playing with ideas, laughing off pain, exposing who we are, and voicing who we desire to be.

The table provides an atmosphere of openness, whether spoken or unspoken, good or bad. But only at the table will individuals expose those emotions. If and how we address topics as they arise makes all the difference in the quality of what we consume and in how full we feel when we walk away from the table.

Chapter 2
Memories and a Meal

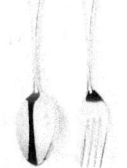

> *We do not remember days;*
> *we remember moments.*
> Cesare Pavese, *The Burning Brand*

As I was growing up, eating at the table created some of the best memories of my life—memories of some really good times and also moments that were not so good. Whether filled with laughter, tears, learning, games, or discussions about a certain TV show, it is clear the table was the focal point for some of the most pivotal moments of my past.

It is amazing how—amid the many hurts, disappointments, and trying times I suffered early in life—I recognized then, as I do now, that the table was the place where nothing seemed to matter at all. In my youthful naiveté, the table represented my safe place. To my young mind, the table was the one place where anyone could share anything without fear of reprisal, and where a person could learn without the threat of being judged or of experiencing the guilt of failure. In a sense, I saw the table as a "no judgment zone" where I could expose my deepest fears and insecurities without feeling naked before the world. At our family table, I could laugh until it hurt, and the refreshment that I experienced would strengthen me for a long time afterwards.

> *I saw the table as a "no judgment zone" where I could expose my deepest fears and insecurities without feeling naked before the world.*

There is one amusing story my mom tells about a morning when she made me eat under the table. The story may seem a little harsh to an outsider, but experiencing the joy of my mom's laughter every time she recounts the details of that funny moment makes it worth hearing it again, despite the potential embarrassment. As the story goes, during breakfast, while living on Nellis Air Force Base in Las Vegas, Nevada, it was my turn at the table to open wide and reveal the contents my mouth had been keeping a secret. Calling my siblings one by one, I would open my mouth wide and expose a mouth full of oatmeal. As a result of my uncontrollable laughter at the sight of their obvious disgust, I would have to struggle to keep from choking. But, not knowing when to answer the curtain call and bring an obnoxious prank to a close, I did not realize my sister had grown tired of my antics.

I guess it was one too many showings because my sister yelled to my mom, who was standing in the kitchen doorway laughing the entire time, trying to maintain her composure as best as she could. Perhaps out of some sense of parental obligation and a stronger desire that I not take this ridiculous practice into my adult years, my mother calmly insisted, "Teddy, if you do it one more time I am going to make you eat your food under the table." I responded as any child would: I said nothing.

Turning back to my sister, I waited for my mom to go back into the kitchen. I then resumed my misguided deed by saying, "Mina, look!!! Gaaaagggg." Again she yelled, "MOM, Talisha won't stop showing her food!" Holding back the laughter, this time my mom said, "Teddy, get your food and sit under the table and eat!" I cannot recall the looks or jesters I made in response to my mother's orders, but knowing me, it was probably as hilarious and annoying as the gagging. Nevertheless, I obeyed and proceeded to my sub-surface restaurant.

So, there I was under the table eating breakfast and using the chair as my tabletop. Just when they thought they had seen the last of me, I tapped a leg... "Mina, look!!! Gaaaagggg." I can still hear the sound of her frustration with me. As my mom retells the story, she says my sister called again, "MOOOOMMMMM!" This is how my mom says my sister would yell in desperation for deliverance from my torment. My mom cracks up every time, as if the entire episode had just happened. She always adds that, even while I was under the table, I was still moving from chair to chair and leg to leg, gagging and laughing, while the only thing she could do was laugh.

Had we not been at our family table, this event might not have been as funny. Memorable maybe, but funny? I doubt it. So, in some ways the table was a refuge and a safe zone. For my siblings I am sure it was the very last place they wanted me to be!

More than a refuge, eating at the table brought us together on many occasions, oftentimes not to eat food at all. I remember the table being the place where we could have family debates. To make things fun and somewhat educational, we would play "Judge and Jury." Someone would have to defend the position for why a particular action should or should not occur. Typically, our parents would play the role of the prosecutor, who would oppose our arguments. Although this game entailed simple lighthearted banter, it did provide me with my first understanding of courtroom procedure and the rules of presenting evidence to defend one's position. From this simple game, I first learned the difference between the terms "sustained" and "overruled." I fondly remember wearing a white raincoat inside out with the black side showing, this being my idea of a judge's robe, and constantly asking my dad: "What does overruled mean and what is sustained again?"

Judge and Jury provided my siblings and me with a quasi-legal framework in which to challenge our parents' decisions without any fear of repercussion. Ultimately, we always knew our parents reserved the right to overrule our arguments or simply throw out our entire case, if they chose to do so. The point is, my parents provided us with a forum to state our position on certain topics and family events.

Without realizing it, we were learning how to state a position and clearly defend our rationale for that position, without being offensive and without being spiteful. The table presented us with a moment to grasp life lessons without the threat of a real conviction or prosecution. For the sake of the game and to keep things fun, my parents minimally exercised their prerogative to overrule. My dad, however, was more liberal in his use of power than was my mother, because he really wanted us to have to work to defend our arguments.

Besides the lessons we learned, eating at the table gave us a family tradition that was far from traditional. To us, it did not matter the activity: just being at the table was all the tradition we needed. Consequently, I can recall on very few occasions my family coming together at the dinner table to enjoy a "traditional" Thanksgiving meal. The only traditional Thanksgiving items I recall us having were turkey, ham, and maybe some pie. Nevertheless, our Thanksgiving celebrations were the absolute best because we were together. It was never a matter of what we had to have; we would cook everything we had and then some. I vividly remember times, while growing up in New Orleans, we would have dishes such as lasagna, deviled eggs, corn, green beans, and peppered steaks with bell peppers over white rice.

Wanting to satisfy everyone's palate on this special day, my mom would simply ask, "What is your favorite dish?" If we had evaporated milk, my little brother would make pecan candy—better than store bought—with or without the pecans, though a pecan tree could be found on any block. Thanksgiving, unlike Christmas, was never really about having all the right stuff; it was the people who mattered most—the right people, the right environment, and the right heart.

Don't get me wrong: we did do Thanksgiving in the traditional sense, but we did not get hung up on whether we could, or would. Christmas on the other hand was sort of a big deal to us—the children that is. As we got older and more selfish, we quickly learned Christmas was not about us and what we thought we should have. Even amidst our selfishness, we learned, fortunately, that receiving a card and cash alone did not take the joy of Christmas away. As for Thanksgiving, we always knew somewhere, someone was cooking, and no one person ever had everything they wanted, at least not at one table. If you wanted the traditional sides and dressings, you would just make your rounds to the homes of family and friends. This to me was tradition. So much so, that even though I do not cook often, I found myself one year recreating my birth family's tradition with my family. We cooked almost everything we could find in the kitchen, according to whatever our various family members wanted to eat.

The greatest thing about our own untraditional Thanksgiving meal was that while we were getting everything together and cooking the meal as a family, I had an opportunity to share these very stories with my children. I was able to revisit a memory of my past and share it with my husband and children while we all stood in the kitchen picking out whatever we could find, laughing, and preparing a meal, creating precious memories of our own.

It is never too soon or too late to begin the process of creating lasting memories that will be treasured for a lifetime. I remember when my son was maybe two or three years old; both my husband and I were in the Air Force at the time. Every Friday was our pizza, wings, and movie night. When I say every Friday, I mean it was *every Friday,* and the only place we would order pizza from was a small shop in Alamogordo, New Mexico, called Dave's Pizza. We ordered so consistently that the employees knew us and would simply pull up our last order. So, we would just order the same thing. There was no other place we would consider. This was our thing; our time; our Fridays.

However, one particular Friday was different. After picking up the pizza and wings and returning home, my husband and I became keenly aware for the first time just how meaningful our pizza, wings, and movie Fridays had become. Out of nowhere, our young son had begun to exhibit a profound exuberance in the days leading up to Friday. As if sensing a changing of the seasons and yet still too young to be able to discern Monday from Tuesday, he somehow sensed when Friday was approaching. His expectations were high and he was so excited this particular Friday that he was practically skipping.

There is one concern I had always thought about but had never voiced, simply because of the possibility of the unspeakable happening. That night we exited our minivan with the pizza in hand and the wings on top as per usual, and then it happened: the wing box slid off of the pizza box straight to the ground, as we all watched in what seemed like slow motion, the wings falling in such a way that they looked as if they were waving goodbye. My son, with the movie in his little hands, looked up at me with his big light brown eyes. He glanced at his father, and dropping his shoulders and throwing his head back, he commenced to wail.

For our son, it was as if the day could not go on and the family time would not be complete because the wings were gone, or shall I say, they went "bye-bye." He had come to know this routine so well that the demise of the wings seemed to have destroyed it all. Somehow, after calming him down and leaving the wings to rest in the driveway, we went forward. From that day on we ensured he knew what family time was really about—even though pizza and wings made family time a little better. At the time, the situation was far from funny—at least to my son who felt the greatest loss and to my husband who was the clumsy culprit. But now we look back and we laugh, over pizza and wings just before we sit down to watch a movie.

Remember: Every meal starts with a desire to be fulfilled. Its aim is to satisfy all who show up to eat, leaving them with more than they possessed when they first arrived, while also instilling in them a desire to return. Whether it is the enjoyment of friends, stories, laughter, memories, pizza, or leftover food—the goal is always to benefit those who show up at your table, causing them to leave better than they came and with a strong desire to return. This daily or weekly ritual at the table should be more than a casual experience or a once-in-a-blue-moon occurrence.

I believe it is deeply embedded in each and every one of us to want to enjoy the manifold blessing of experiences that take place around the table, whether or not we know it, or care to admit, or wish to surrender to this fact. We are a people who want more, who desire better, and who hope to be remembered. Each and every day, the issues of life challenge us to define who we truly are, and there is absolutely no better place to be you than in the company of family and friends, all together in one place—hopefully at the table.

Each and every day, the issues of life challenge us to define who we truly are, and there is absolutely no better place to be you than in the company of family and friends, all together in one place—hopefully at the table.

Chapter 3
Words Matter

A picture can tell a thousand words, but a few words can change its story.

Sebastyne Young

Memories are awesome to have, but it is the words in those memories that determine whether those mental photographs will be a legacy of blessings or a cloud of gloom for the person who must carry them around for an entire lifetime. Words are life. Words shape the essence of who we are, whether good or bad. Nathaniel Hawthorne captured the purity of words so eloquently when he stated: "Words—so innocent and powerless as they are, as standing in a dictionary, how

> *"Words—so innocent and powerless as they are, as standing in a dictionary, how potent for good and evil they become in the hands of one who knows how to combine them."*

There may be times when we simply sit back and consider the use and misuse of words by others, especially when the words are directed toward us. However, when it comes to the things we say, rarely do we consider our own use and misuse of words—those targeted at others and at ourselves. There are words we want to hear, but only from a particular person or a select group of individuals. Likewise, an individual on the receiving end of your words holds the same hope, as well as the same prejudice.

For me, hearing from my parents was always important. I am sure they never knew it, but it was. There was not much my parents would discourage me from doing, as long as it was legal and had clearly defined ethical boundaries. I also grew up on a diet of harsh words from extended family members and friends, words like "that's stupid," or "you're a stupid girl" or "dummy," or hearing "shut up" on a constant basis. I never ascribed any evil intentions to their words. Instead, I always figured their comments were kind-hearted joking. After all, these were people I cared about and who cared about me, I thought. I felt the heart of the individual saying the negative things and the relationship we had were more important than the words themselves, at least where family and friends were concerned.

It was not until my teenage years that I first noticed just how important my parents' positive and affirming words were in shaping my self-esteem and providing me with a protective barrier to ward off the harmful effects of the negative insults hurled in my direction. Some of my parents' words became goals towards which I would aspire, while others were images of what I should not become. Either way, I valued their words, even when I may not have shown it.

For many years I was a member of school dance teams, and competitions and performances became important to me. Often my parents could not attend events in which I participated and I understood why. Yet, I found myself at times fighting hard not to hold it against them. There were times I would gesture as though it did not matter at all. In actuality, it did matter and it did hurt that they could not attend. Instead of showing how I truly felt, I would simply tuck my feelings in the back of my mind because of our family dynamic, and because of the things I felt my parents would say if they knew my thoughts.

During events, I would look around inconspicuously to see if at least one of them had shown up. The presence of a parent gave me a sense of confidence in what I was doing, which always made me perform a little better. I did not boost my performance because I wanted to show off. Rather, I simply wanted to show my parents I was becoming the person they constantly assured me I was: a young woman who could do anything she set out to accomplish and one who could do it well. I wanted them to be proud of the fact that their efforts concerning me were paying off. I simply wanted to share my special moments with them.

> *When you know that someone will celebrate you with their presence and with their words of encouragement, those gestures have the ability to draw the best out of you.*

When you know that someone will celebrate you with their presence and with their words of encouragement, those gestures have the ability to draw the best out of you.

For me, those precious moments at home, particularly those around the table, when we were all together were when my parents' words created unforgettable mental pictures of the person I truly am, and gave me clear images of the kind of life I should enjoy. Their words painted images of my life as it could be, and as it should be. What they depicted for me was a life to be desired and realized.

I saw myself as a great entrepreneur because of the opportunities my father gave me to make money by bringing work home and paying me to do small tasks. Additionally, I saw myself as a great friend because my mom saw this quality in me and she used every opportunity at her disposal to reinforce it. She would often talk about my willingness to give; therefore, I always saw myself as a willing giver. Whether my giving was of time, money, encouragement, or just a listening ear, I became a giver because I saw in me what my mother reinforced. I became a giver, and a great one at that.

I have since had the opportunity to speak with my mother concerning what I do now and what I did growing up. I asked her if she ever imagined me in the accounting profession because of the small tasks and extra things I would do in order to make money. To my surprise, she said, "No." She then added, "Everything you did was to help people, even when you did work for your father."

She went on to say my efforts back then were never for the sake of any profession; she said my commitment to others stemmed simply from a sincere desire to help. Furthermore, she shared that even when I did earn money, I immediately set out to do something for someone else. My mother joked I could often be found giving away items belonging to the family. As she shared, all I could think was, "WOW!" I am very grateful for what she saw and still sees in me, but I am even more grateful she continues to speak powerful words of encouragement into my life, despite the fact I am now an adult with children of my own.

I remember a particular incident in elementary school, near the Thanksgiving holiday when we participated in an annual food drive. (What is it with Thanksgiving and my family?) Anyhow, every student was asked to bring in canned goods to support the event and to help the cause. Like many of the students and faculty, upon hearing the announcement, I did my part and brought in a can of food. I must have gotten carried away at the prospect of giving away stuff, no doubt bearing out the words my mother shared with me about being a giver. The next day, I hid three or four cans of food in my backpack and then set off to school. Full of pride, I presented my offering to the teacher. Obviously enjoying the feeling of exceeding the basic requirement, I found myself over the next few weeks stashing canned goods in my backpack until the food drive was over.

My proudest moment came when I heard my name announced over the school's PA system: I was the top giver! Sweet! Huh? It was. When my mom found out—rather than admonishing me for sneaking from our home what, in the end, amounted to fifty-two cans of food—she encouraged me and assured me I had done a good thing. My brother, on the other hand, did not see it the same way. He commented, "We're going to need to get food from them, since Talisha gave all of ours away." Truth be told, we did not have much left for ourselves after my overreaching act of generosity, but this situation and my mother's reply showed I was simply conforming to the image she had of me. I became an embodiment of her very words and we never found ourselves lacking when it came to food.

Who is feeding you words, and what words are you confirming and conforming to? Whether at a physical table or the table of life to feed on words or a meal prepared in love, or to play card games or just be together in one room, coming together with family, friends, and others who influence your life and actions should be important—dare I say, a priority. Make it important, and ensure it is a time to share, laugh, and learn. I really believe, in the family I grew up in, and now in my own family, we found a treasure in simply being together. We are often found laughing at each other, ourselves, or total strangers. We genuinely enjoy each other's company. We aim to make every moment together as memorable as possible.

In fact, when we go to the movies, we no longer watch the movie just to be entertained. We ask questions, we make points, we quiz, and we even play a game we call "What movie is this from?", where we re-enact scenes of a movie. We also get our children's opinions on different aspects of the movie, which reveals to my husband and I their individual thought patterns and their possible reactions to situations they may encounter in life. Clearly, we recognize they do not know everything, but we know we are responsible for teaching them everything we know. Can they learn by what we do? Yes. But when we communicate to them verbally certain things, the teaching moments we want to reinforce get sealed in their hearts and in their minds.

We have come to understand the value of words to the point where we want to make sure our words are the ones which speak loudest, are most influential, are balanced, and are the truth. We want our words to shape the lives and characters of our children more than what they hear on the radio, see on television, or are filled with at school. How do we do it? We allow them to speak and have a voice, but they, on the other hand, are required to listen.

We have come to understand the value of words to the point where we want to make sure our words are the ones which speak loudest, are most influential, are balanced, and are the truth.

Understanding that words create pictures, we are very careful what we say, how we say it, or when we say certain things around and about our children. We are so particular about the messages we communicate to our kids, the words "shut up" took years to be said. I know this may sound crazy; however, I also know the sting words can carry, even words we use casually. Because I've found that certain words can teach one how to react to a person or situation, my goal has been to teach my children how to respond; especially how to respond intelligently and with control and not react at the point of frustration or out of offense.

I believe coming together at the table should allow family members to speak candidly, but with respect. Our children can be open and understand boundaries. We can laugh, joke, and play, while maintaining an atmosphere of mutual respect. One thing we instill is: You do not change who you are when in public. Teach your children the integrity that goes along with being exactly who they are, whether at home or in public. Trust the environment that you set at home will follow you no matter where you go.

On many occasions we have witnessed how some parents overreact by chastening their children's behavior in public, while overlooking or condoning the same behavior in the home. This type of inconsistency not only confuses the child, but also sends the message that there is a certain way one should act at home and another way to act in public. If your child talks back at home, he or she is on course to do the same thing in a store. If your daughter rolls her eyes and has an attitude because she cannot have her way, you cannot overreact when she does it in public. If your son stomps his feet and falls out at home because he wants something and you find yourself giving in to his demands, more than likely he will throw a temper tantrum in the candy aisle in expectation of the same outcome he got at home.

I believe what we allow at home should not shock or embarrass us when we leave home. You are who you are, no matter where you are. And even when you are pretending to be someone you are not, the real you is bound to show up, sooner or later. This goes for both parents and children alike. Consider the fact that the home is our training ground, and the place we spend time together with our children is our classroom, and the time we use to pass along important life lessons to our children is our time of instruction. For once our children venture off into the public domain, the important exams will take place. If you have cultivated an environment where honest dialogue can take place, then the table will become the central hub where everyone will gather for after-action review.

Every parent desires for their children to live by the words they have shared. Good or bad, purposeful or unintended, it is our words and not our actions alone that feed the spirit of our children. How then, if time is never made for teaching to take place, do we hold them to a standard they were never taught? Consider the words used and the source of the words spoken. We all thrive on the words spoken to us daily. It remains the parents' responsibility to be the filter to ensure our children are receiving only life-producing, success-directed words which will encourage them along the path of their prescribed destiny. We should endeavor to be the loudest voice our children hear. Our voices must ring so loudly in their ears that they can hear us even when we are not present with them. Our voice must be clear enough to reach out and touch them so they feel compelled to follow our instructions, even when we are not standing over their shoulders.

Be the voice that echoes every dream God gave them, the eyes that see the paths they should take, the comforting hands to shape their self-esteem, the legs to assist them to venture off into to the world on their own, the ears that carefully safeguard what they hear, and the protector who uproots whatever and whoever is not assigned to bless their lives. Not only should we eat at the table to create an environment where the free exchange of ideas takes place, but our lives should also be the very table from which our children can glean those important life lessons that will send them off into the world equipped with the tools necessary to be successful.

We must all come to a point in life where we review our lives, no matter how good or bad, and realize that before we can set the table for our children and others who depend on us, we all will need a moment to set the table for ourselves. We have to figure out where we are sourcing the "food" we will feed others and how to prepare both ourselves and our words at the table, which is our life, and feed them without prejudice and "cook" without compromise and the holding back of all truth, all disappointments, and all rewards.

Chapter 4
Who's Feeding You?

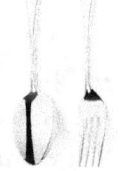

Just because someone talks, does not make them qualified to speak. Just because you hear them, does not mean you have to listen.

Talisha Bennett

As I sit at the table of life, I often wonder how different my life would be had my parents not given me encouraging words to live by. I wonder if I would have accepted at face value the countless negative words directed my way as a child. Would I have turned out like so many people I have met, individuals who wander through life experimenting with this and dabbling in that, remaining nowhere long enough to consume anything that provides stability and direction? You know, "Eat the meat and spit out the bones?" Knowing how naïve and gullible I was back then, I probably would have choked on bones while spitting out the meat of honest conversations, simply to appease so-called friends who did not have my best interests at heart.

Have you ever given careful thought to the idiom, "Eat the meat and spit out the bones?" Whenever I heard this quote, I would ask myself, "How much will you eat before you accidentally swallow a bone?" Do not misunderstand me; I believe there is a great deal of truth and wisdom packed into this short saying. However, I still wonder what it actually means. Does it suggest we should accept the beneficial substance of what a person says, while refusing to take in those harmful and irrelevant aspects of their message? Or, does it mean we should eat what is good for us, but spit out the portions that can kill us?

Every time you engage in conversation or simply listen to a person speak—whether his or her message is valid or not—you are being programmed to some degree by the words you hear. How then do you determine what words to take in and what to dismiss? Having the ability to discern both the type and quality of information you should embrace is the key to knowing where to go to get the proper diet of information to support your life's journey.

You are the only one qualified to determine what words you should or should not embrace based upon your unique purpose here on Earth. You must be able to distinguish between all the possible voices out there: the ones to whom you should give attention and those you should ignore. Have you learned to distinguish between the voices?

Clearly we all find ourselves searching for answers in life. The danger is in not knowing what you are searching for. Yes, you can eat the meat and spit out the bones, but what happens when eating too much of the wrong thing changes your appetite, so that what was once detestable to your intellectual sensibilities is now not only appealing, but preferred? What happens when you feel as though the meat is no longer satisfying? What if the bones begin to resemble the meat so much you can no longer distinguish one from the other? Such is the delicate predicament of our children, absent our consistent and loving guidance.

Without our attentive oversight, each voice our child hears can seem like the one with the right answers. Because young children are initially so trusting of any and everyone who enters their world, they are most vulnerable to the many voices out there with no other aim than to mislead them. This is why parents must serve as vigilant gatekeepers for all of what our children do, view, and hear, especially in those early formative years.

We all want relationships and the feeling of belonging, and we all in some way desire to be led and mentored. Moreover, we all want to come into our own as responsible individuals. Without qualified people in our lives to ensure we hear the right words, we tend to gravitate in the direction of words that may seem right for the moment, or come only from individuals within our own culture. Without ears that have been tutored by qualified individuals so that we are able to question the many voices that come in and out of our lives, we have no way to properly distinguish between those voices that are right for us and those that are almost right. Most of the words we receive from others are not sturdy enough to support our aspirations; neither

> *Most of the words we receive from others are not sturdy enough to support our aspirations; neither are they enriched with the proper nutrients to cause growth in our lives.*

are they enriched with the proper nutrients to cause growth in our lives.

Most people are only interested in being fed; they do not care who does the feeding. We can find ourselves plagued with the serious condition of "itching ears," where we go running to and fro seeking those who speak only what we want to hear and are willing to adhere to. Worse yet, we can find ourselves wanting more and more, never satisfied with the balanced meal put before us. In this particular case, individuals are always living with an appetite for something greater than what is being served, gluttonous for more without regard for the meal that has already been consumed.

This brings to mind a particular chicken restaurant I like going to for lunch every now and then with my husband. I absolutely love their barbeque pulled pork sandwich. I love it so much that I will order it every time, even though it is hit or miss as to whether or not they will prepare it just right, thinking maybe this time it will be prepared the way I like it. Sometimes the bread is just right, but I may only get a sample-sized serving of the barbecued pulled pork. There have been times I have gotten a hefty portion of the barbecued pulled pork. In such cases, I have to eat it with a fork just so I can enjoy a tasty balance of bread and meat together. Then there have been times when the barbecued pork serving was really good but the bread was hard. Nevertheless, I find myself going back time and time again, and each time I hold out the hope that maybe this time the food will be prepared to my liking. On very few occasions have I ever had my order turn out just right, but these are the very few occasions that keep me returning again and again.

I recall one day in particular, for it was like no other day I had ever experienced. For some strange reason, I just had to have that sandwich for lunch. No, seriously, I just *had* to. If you have ever been pregnant or have spent time with an expectant mother, you know there are times when the craving for something is so strong the person will drive all over town at two o'clock in the morning just to satisfy that craving. This is how badly I wanted that sandwich.

So, my husband and I pulled up to the restaurant and I placed my order. This time, however, the thought of things going wrong was far from my mind. When we got the food I still had no bad thoughts—just hunger. The smell of the barbecue invited me to dive in while we drove to our office. Although I was very tempted, I held off. I wanted to be able to enjoy my lunch without having to focus on my husband's driving or being rushed to take a bite between bumps in the road.

As we pulled into the parking lot of our building, we parked on the side as usual. My anticipation of this meal was overwhelming. It was as if I had not eaten in weeks. To top things off, it had been a while since I last had this sandwich. As usual there was too much meat, which is fine with me. So, I grabbed my fork and dug in. Layer one, gone. It tasted like it had been drugged with an overdose of barbecue sauce, but I ate it anyway. Fighting off the thoughts of my past encounters, I continued, taking into account that the balance has more to do with the bread than with the meat and sauce alone.

At this point, I proceeded on to the second layer. The barbecued pulled pork was tasty, just the way I liked it. Full steam ahead! I began a major assault on the third layer. But after about two jabs, my fork came to a screeching halt, blocked by something I had never encountered in all my years of eating this sandwich. The culprit? You guessed it: a bone.

All previous bad experience with this meal paled in comparison to the obstruction in the middle of my sandwich because I could have died if I had swallowed that bone. If I had known this was a likely possibility, I probably would have stopped eating from the restaurant a long time ago. Or would I?

Most people would conclude that fifty-three bad dining experiences out of a total of seventy-two visits constitutes a dining establishment unworthy of a return visit. So, why, you may ask, would I continue to go back to a restaurant where I get satisfactory service less than fifty percent of the time? I reasoned that the few times when the food was prepared perfectly more than compensated for the many times it was not. However, when I saw the bone staring up at me, I got the picture and concluded that I had had enough. This incident was the proverbial line in the sand. Once I crossed it, I would not look back. I figured I would either choose another item on the menu or choose a totally different place to eat.

> *The main difference between the service you get at a restaurant and the people you encounter daily is that the restaurant service will be spot-on much of the time, whereas one hundred percent of the people you deal with daily will possess flaws and imperfections.*

I share this story simply to say this same concept applies when it comes to dealing with people. The main difference between the service you get at a restaurant and the people you encounter daily is that the restaurant service will be spot-on much of the time, whereas one hundred percent of the people you deal with daily will possess flaws and imperfections. Knowing this, you must learn which people you should go to for the information, guidance, and mentorship you need, because not everyone is qualified to provide you those things which can propel you forward, faster in life.

The quality of the information you take in will be determined largely by the people you allow to speak into your life. You feed on words just as much as you feed on food. Think for a moment about why you decide to go to a particular friend or family member's house for the holidays. We all have that favorite home we like to visit and the infamous one we wish to avoid. Our preference is not always based on who prepares the best holiday meal. To be quite honest, there are just some people who are not very pleasant to be around. Their mere presence sets you off for one reason or another. We can receive invite after invite, yet we will find every reason to turn down the invitation.

> *The quality of the information you take in will be determined largely by the people you allow to speak into your life.*

The same care should be taken regarding your life and the information you allow into it. There are foods you will not eat, and there are some foods you are willing to try. If you do not like a particular food item, more than likely you will refuse it the next time it is offered to you, or simply push it to one side of your plate. Why then, when it comes to people, do we allow them to feed us things we do not need or want? Instead, we entertain their words by sitting down at their tables to eat. How soon before the bone is bitten will we muster the courage to refuse them altogether? Some people you have to toss or set aside, just like a bad plate of food from your favorite aunt whom you, and everyone else in the family, know cannot cook. You may take a nibble or a small sample of the food, but like everyone else, you are already convinced that full consumption of the meal will do major internal damage.

At whose table are you sitting? Eat at a table that will nourish you; do not wait until you choke on something never meant for you to ingest. When searching for people to pour into your life, always qualify them by closely observing the quality of their lifestyle, or by paying attention to the quality of the people with whom they surround themselves. Consumption from the wrong people, television shows, songs, podcasts, or books can be more of a detriment to you and your future than not being fed at all. It is easier to fill an empty pot than to fill and flush out a pot that is already soiled with baked-on dirt. If you disregard who is feeding you (or in this case your children), you will soon find yourself and your children full, but only on stuff that will not carry you to your desired destination in life.

Chapter 5

Pounding Crumbs into Bread

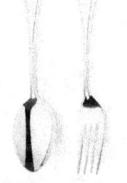

I am not interested in picking up crumbs of compassion thrown from the table of someone who considers himself my master. I want the full menu of rights.

Bishop Desmond Tutu

From childhood until well into our adult years, we must battle so many things in our lives. If a proper foundation is never laid for us to stand upon, or necessary affirmation is not provided to inspire us to keep going, we will live our lives feasting upon the crumbs that fall from the tables of complete strangers. If we are not careful, we can find ourselves soaking up every word served to us, whether true or not, all because we do not know what we want, need, or should have. The only thing we can figure out with any certainty is there is something more we yearn to obtain. And when we are uncertain of our identity, we will be content to live out our existence accepting life's handouts.

We will rarely stop to consider whether the words doled out to us by others are suitable for our particular mandates. We just know we need to hear words. As a result, we end up making one mistake after another. Before you know it, the consequences of our poor decision-making become part of our daily diet of frustration and discouragement.

We have collected the measly crumbs that have fallen from the lips of every childhood friend and every teacher who has ever told us who we were not (or would never

> *We have collected the measly crumbs that have fallen from the lips of every childhood friend and every teacher who has ever told us who we were not (or would never become), and we have pounded these crumbs into a form that has become our own self-image.*

become), and we have pounded these crumbs into a form that has become our own self-image. We wear this false self-image as though it is who we are, and we go off into the world assuming we are properly dressed and adorned to tackle the issues of life. However, life's trials will soon reveal we are not properly equipped to face life's challenges at all.

A nurturing table—around which we would consistently gather and collect vital truth, solid teaching, and character-building encouragement—would teach us early on the difference between crumbs and a meal. We would develop an appetite for the properly seasoned words that loving parents know how to bring to the right temperature for the proper feeding of their children. Around such a table, we would feel self-assured based upon the careful preparation of our parents' warm words rather than the empty words from strangers who could care less whether or not we ate a balanced meal.

Low self-esteem would not be welcome in our lives because constant encouragement would be the meal of the day. In fact, it would be too uncomfortable to stand in our presence because we are convinced of our worth, even before venturing out into the world. In sitting at such a table, we would learn what constitutes true fulfillment versus that which is fleeting; like freshly baked bread served on plates of righteousness and offered from hands of those who honor us, words of esteem flow from the lips of loving parents and caring friends.

Eventually we all get to a point in life where the crumbs can no longer sustain our aspirations, and we can no longer maintain our false pretenses. But, when all we have collected in life is all we know of ourselves, we fight hard to hold onto the mere crumbs we have come to rely upon, constantly pounding them into someone else's image of us. It is these crumbs—represented by the words of unqualified individuals—that we pound into the dry loaf of who we think we are. Over the years we find ourselves molding and shaping that loaf into a hardened mass with our tears of uncertainty and regret. Desperately, we collect more crumbs to continue to build more of who we are not, all because no one ever told us who we really are.

We walk around leaving trails of ourselves behind, and we are then left wondering why all the wrong people seem to find us. Never do we stop to realize we are merely a crusted roll of who everyone else has told us we should be, never having a true image to which we can conform. Had we just sat at the table, one meal could have deflated our egos to the proper levels and filled us with humility. One spoonful of truth would have shown us who we truly are, and would have crystallized an image in our minds, giving us the right dreams to pursue.

Truth, well-prepared and fed to us, would have taught us how to cut away and separate ourselves from people who have no place in our lives, without ripping them apart or leaving portions of ourselves connected to them. A proper meal of truth would have even taught us to identify and cut away undesired personality traits we find in ourselves.

One sip of ice water in a tall glass would have shown us how to handle both sensitive and cold-hearted individuals, revealing that which should be preserved versus that which should be completely severed. One sitting in the presence of wise parents or guardians would have revealed the importance of having authority figures in our lives, providing us with an understanding for the respect that comes with waiting our turn to be seated, seen, and heard.

At the table we would also have learned how to move forward in life without bumping and disrupting others. At the same time, we would have been taught how to sit and maintain a dignified posture even in the midst of the most humiliating circumstances, exposing to us that the ability to rise above whatever comes our way is already embedded within us. We would have understood how to dress discreetely in modest apparel in order to respect the body beneath the clothes. We would never have settled for the crumbs that fell from the laps of those who sit in wait to devour precious lives so full of potential. Why settle for crumbs when the table has an entire smorgasbord of menu options? Now, the choice is truly yours. How you see yourself will determine your position; and how you present yourself will determine the position others think you should have.

We must determine in our hearts that we are worth more. In all that life has given and in all it has to offer, why continue to settle for less? Why continue to settle at all? What are you truly worth? If you have no table to eat at and no one to pour words into you, decide to make it your life's mission to pour into yourself until you can identify a qualified mentor to speak into your life. Say the right things, read the right books, hear the right music, and see the right pictures. Be mindful of everything you take in because your future depends on it.

The more words you hear that are right and life-building, the easier it becomes to weed out the wrong words and the people who deliver them. Before you set out on your journey, release your past, forgive your foes, embrace your family, honor your friends, starve your doubts, stand up to your fears, and declare to the world that you are here to stake your claim to joy and abundance in all of their manifestations.

The more words you hear that are right and life-building, the easier it becomes to weed out the wrong words and the people who deliver them.

Proclaim who you really are. It is now your time to come forward boldly so that the people who are designed to speak into your life can give you what you need to succeed and declare your true identity, even if the truth they share will at times hurt your feelings.

Sometimes the best thing is to accept who and where you are in life. I often tell my children to just "own it." If you own it, then at least you will have a starting point. Now shake off the crumbs and proceed to move forward. Know you are not your past. You are not your hurt. You are not a failure, nor are you your failures. There is hope. Beauty is embedded in you, and you must do all you can to let it show forth. THERE IS GREATNESS IN YOU!

Consider the attributes of freshly baked bread: the aroma, the warmth, the delicateness of its core. Now consider the process it endures before becoming the finished product that can be enjoyed. We are a standing bowl of many ingredients and a mixture of additives that take away from our inherent nutritional value. But I have GOOD NEWS. Unlike bread, we can be prepared all over again without having to be thrown out or tossed to the side. Even if we have come to our end, we must know we are worth more. If you are at that point, then you are nearer to the place of a turnaround than you can possibly imagine.

When you are at the point where you sincerely desire a radical change in the direction of your life, you are at the point of discovering who you truly are. This critical moment holds more promise than the combined total of all of your prior years. You do not have to recreate yourself or try to redefine who you are. Simply discover the true essence of your creation. You are better served when you are whole and complete. And you are valued more by your content than by your décor.

Chapter 6
Prepared to Be Served

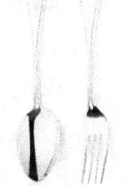

Nothing is better for self-esteem than survival.
       Martha Gellhorn

We all experience a vast range of unsettling ordeals throughout life. Yet, seldom do we ever stop to consider why we find ourselves in certain predicaments, let alone ask ourselves for what purpose these circumstances are preparing us. Overwhelmed by the cares of life, most people are unable to simply live in the moment and embrace the many lessons these various life circumstances have come to teach us.

I often think about the many rigors my son endures in order to hone his skills as a gymnast.

Because of his youth and immaturity, typically he does not appreciate the foundation-building process required to take an individual from very fundamental routines to those movements requiring greater degrees of difficulty. As a beginner he brought to the sport a very high level of physical athleticism, and consequently he did not have to focus much of his attention on the fundamentals and mechanics of foundational exercises. Oftentimes he fails to appreciate the role these basics serve in producing strength, stamina, and agility. To him, a hand stand is simply that: an exercise he was able to do even before he took up the sport of gymnastics. His coach, however, sees things from an entirely different perspective.

From the coach's standpoint, tremendous talent means nothing if it does not rest on a sub-structure of solid fundamentals. While my son thinks it may be cool and impressive to be able to do hand stands, his coach recognizes this basic skill is simply preparation for the more difficult apparatus routines down the line, which will place a heavier demand on his entire skill-set. Therefore, my young son would be wise to pay close attention during the foundation-laying stages of his development, recognizing that more difficult conditions lie ahead.

His greatest challenge is fighting through the unceasing correction and boredom of constantly rehearsing movements he feels he has already mastered. Since he does not have the coach's perspective, he is not able to run ahead of the coach's instructions and he often wrestles with frustration and confusion. At times, he feels as though he is much further along in his development than his coach's assessment may suggest. However, he must learn to take every bit of instruction and difficult-to-swallow correction as an opportunity to grow and improve.

> *Learn to take every bit of instruction and difficult-to-swallow correction as an opportunity to grow and improve.*

When I sense his focus is drifting away from where it should be, I simply say to him, "Somewhere, someone is training harder." Usually, my motto is all that is needed to get him to refocus. He then figures if someone is working harder (whether he sees them or not), their work will one day become his major competition.

How often do we face difficult situations and conclude our world is crumbling around us and everything is coming to an end? Rarely do we see those defining moments for the destiny-altering, character-building, circumstances they truly are. Typically, we do not see past our present trials to recognize the actual renovation and construction taking place within our lives. As we mature, we are able to look back to see certain trials were necessary to help us arrive at a much better place.

I think of the many people who choose to end their lives every day, all because they have experienced such prolonged distress and despair; they conclude deliverance from their predicaments will never come. I have heard it said we should never make permanent decisions based on temporary circumstances. As with the passage of each season, we must know, "this too shall pass."

I am sure at this point, those readers who have ever experienced a major setback are probably saying, "You don't understand; if you had gone through what I've experienced, you wouldn't be making such assertions." I appreciate and understand your sentiments. However, because you have arrived at this point in the book, recognize you have indeed survived all that has happened to you thus far. Know your breakthrough victory is just beyond these pages: begin to envision brighter tomorrows. I dare you to choose to picture it!

I have experienced certain mind-numbing events in my own life. If I were to share just a few of them, you would quickly realize I can definitely identify with the hurt, pain, suicidal thoughts, loss, or fear of whatever ordeal you may be experiencing currently. I do not have to be or have ever been in your exact condition or situation to be able to understand how you may be feeling. Whether I understand what you have gone through or not has absolutely nothing to do with the healing process you need to experience behind what you have suffered.

I can recall at around age eight or nine years old, leaving a note in my desk which exclaimed, "I WISH I WAS DEAD." This was during the time when searching a student's desk was expected. I received a visit from social workers that weekend—the very weekend, unbeknownst to me, my mother was planning to visit the grave of my brother, Kendrick. My brother died of crib death only a few months before my conception. My mother was left with having to forego the visit to Kenny's grave to sit through rounds of family questioning because of my note and obvious despair. Her response to this situation may have been the one thing that saved my life.

Years later, at sixteen years old, I got pregnant. I was only a junior in high school, and I was so terrified of having to break the news to the baby's father. My heart shattered in a million little pieces, hearing him say, "It's a lie." Never mind the fact I still had my own family to tell. Somehow, I summoned the courage to tell my mother on a ferry boat ride to visit with my aunt, while my older brother sat in the car with us. First of all, I knew there were too many people around for her to throw me overboard, and secondly, I knew my brother would not let her kill me. Months later, I was rushed to the hospital after miscarrying at home, while using the restroom.

I can still vividly see those tiny hands, waving as if to say goodbye. I also remember the haunting memory of seeing those dark circles where eyes were forming, just looking at me. I was just coming to the end of my first trimester. To this very day, I continue to live with the stinging loss of my virginity taken from me at age thirteen, and the loss of a precious life my sixteen-year-old body was ill-equipped to bring to term. And for the second time in my life, I wrestled with the thought of suicide because I saw it as the only escape from the predicament in which I found myself.

Like countless others, I wish I did not have a story like this to tell, but I do. I can either allow it to imprison me for the rest of my life, or I can share it with someone who cannot see past the pain of a similar situation to move forward. This is the story of my life. I can choose to throw it away and hide it as though it never happened, or I can offer my testimony for the benefit of providing hope to someone else, so they might be encouraged to go on living.

I know a young woman who, in her youth, experienced devastation so deep, she describes her unsettling pain and loneliness as feeling as though the world was shifting and closing in on her. Full of emotions and yet too young to comprehend what she was experiencing, she chose to cope by burying the pain of the traumatizing events deep within her past. She could not, for the life of her, recall the lessons of the table. It was as if the tables had turned and the honesty, integrity, and transparency embodied in the table discussions were nowhere to be found. She knew there was going to be a major shift in her family life because of the things that had transpired. Every memory was re-evaluated for its genuineness. Moments were now defined by the trauma of what had happened. Every hug, every laugh, and every touch were now a cause for suspicion. To this day, she often says she will never be able to put every painful detail of what happened into words. She also feels this painful story is not hers alone to tell.

She revealed that she had lived for years under the crushing weight of a painful past, feeling as though she was in it alone. Her isolation was magnified because of the conflicting burden of having to shelter the sins of her family from the shame of public scrutiny. She described how she felt—as though she was merely living life as an extra in a movie absent of any narration. Over the many years of hiding in the shadows of a very painful secret, she perfected the skill of ad-libbing so she would be able to blend into the dialogue of any scene in which she found herself, without the truth of her past ever being detected. For many years, she was successful at preserving the secret and her family, while also keeping the possibility of her emotional healing at bay. Decades of hurt fed the ocean of anger and bitterness she kept bottled up inside. She nurtured an emotional divide so wide she learned to love from a distance, seldom letting anyone in.

As with so many, her hurt did not stop there. She exposed to me how short stays with family became superficial choruses of hellos and goodbyes, leaving her to keep buried deep within the devastating secret of witnessing childhood molestation. She did this perfectly for years.

Locking the pain of these memories within was her unconscious way of locking the rest of the world out. Secrets and emotional detachment from others became the story of her life, yet all the while continuing in her hurt and in hurting others along the way. Her life, like mine, became one of tightly held secrets and throbbing wounds, which were the evidence of our continued existence. The feeling of pain became proof we were still alive, though we were dying inside.

It would be ludicrous and naïve to think that no family or individual has gone through challenges or heart-wrenching events in life. It is at those distressing times when the table's true value shines through the most. The table is indeed the place where security is found and freedom is waiting. If never addressed or exposed, our ailing pasts will produce festering wounds which never heal—oozing and seeping traces of the very issues that are the essence of their origins. Left unattended for long, the resulting behaviors become just as destructive as the initial acts that created them.

We must consider that sexual abuse of any kind, especially at the hands of a close family member, is rarely isolated to one occurrence. Outcomes may differ, but one generation of abuse is typically passed along to the next generation.

It can be covered up and masked on the outside, but the victim's actions and reactions will often display all the obvious signs that something has taken place. Take for example a carbonated beverage: if shaken too long without any room for a controlled and slow release, the contents inside will explode in order to find relief from the pressure build-up, creating a mess everywhere and on everyone in close proximity.

In the case of this particular individual, she managed to get through her ordeals. Without telling people all the details of what transpired in her life, she has helped others who have experienced and witnessed similar devastation. She confronted thoughts of suicide and considered its effect on the lives of those who were connected to her. Once she looked outside of her hurt, she saw a glimpse of the beautiful person she truly is, and she was determined to find her worth. No longer does shame haunt her, neither does guilt nag her. In the midst of her struggles, she found the strength to overcome the shame of her past. She now enjoys a life worth living. So must you!

> *Live so we can be inspired by your story!*

Find a reason to press forward in the face of all the adversity you have experienced. There are so many others in similar circumstances who will draw inspiration when you tell them how you have overcome. Therefore, live so we can be inspired by your story!

Chapter 7
Life Made to Order

*It is your reaction to adversity,
not the adversity itself that determines
how your life's story will develop.*
Dieter F. Uchtdorf

Sitting at the table should prepare us for the world. So, regardless of our past or present situation—good, bad or indifferent—we must choose to reroute the current course of our lives and return to the place where the fuse to our precious dreams was first ignited: at the table. The table can provide us with the vital nutrients that build character and self-esteem, nutrients that we need to succeed in the world. Before this can happen, the individuals who sit at the table must first identify and deal with certain issues of their past. Otherwise, parents with unresolved hurts and anxieties will unknowingly pass along the effects of those issues to their children, thus preventing precious dreams from being created.

The table is the one constant in every home; it always radiates with the potential to give life. However, the people who pull up to it to be fed are not always so steady. In homes where families no longer flock to the tables—once venues of great fellowship, guidance, and instruction—rest assured that the people have changed, not the table. This is certainly the case when the table has become a place that family members avoid altogether.

The many facets of life can take a tremendous toll on all of us in ways that zap us of our willingness to return to tables we, at one time, never wanted to leave. The hurts we sustain as a result of what has been done to us, either by someone outside the home, or inside, will certainly temper our desire to revisit the table as a willing and enthusiastic participant.

When hurts and offenses go untended, the individuals who carry them around will soon see the table and its occupants through tainted lenses. And though the people may be able to pick up and go on with their lives, affected the most is the precious table, which has become another discarded, rarely used fixture in the home, one that no one regards with respect or views the same way.

If we can start with simply owning our past and all that comes with it, regardless of fault and guilt, we can confess our faults to one another so true healing can begin to take place. We have to decide whether we want to live in the pain of our past or the possibilities of our future, sorting out the pieces as we go. We should take the approach of Jonathan Winters who said, "I couldn't wait for success, so I went ahead without it." This was my approach to obtaining the healing I desperately needed. I refused to wait for things to be "just right" in me before moving on in life. I had to confess the mistakes of my past, own them, and then work toward getting over some painful memories just so I could press forward. Yes, it happened, and as in the case of so many others, I had family issues to contend with. The table played a vital role, but it was not the foundation.

> *We have to decide whether we want to live in the pain of our past or the possibilities of our future, sorting out the pieces as we go.*

Rather, it was the place where I went to get the foundation established.

Now, I am older and strong enough to handle truth and choose the company I keep. Once I find myself alone and seated at the table of my own thoughts, I realize I no longer need my father or mother to call me to the table because I gather there now of my own accord, bringing all of me. I am able now to look back and survey the many winding turns and unintended detours that my life took to get me to where I am today. I can see how the pain of my past has gripped me and, in turn, how I have allowed it to paralyze the efforts of others through me. I can still feel the pain of loss, which remains with me to this very day. I can dig up the seeds sown and planted to change me. I see images of a past so dark I can feel the weight of the choices made for me, and the choices made because of me, and by me. As I sit at the table, I am joined by a hope that celebrates the fact I am here where I belong.

Instead of hurt, I choose healing. Whether I truly ever understand it all or not, I cannot continue to entwine my future with the past and believe I can possibly ever start over that way. I can no longer afford to give my shame a seat at the head of the table, while my pride quietly serves us. I have determined my table will not be, from this point forward, adorned by things from my past. It will no longer hold the bittersweet refreshments of painful memories, which keep my focus in the rear view mirror of life. Neither will I allow any more space for pity parties that leave no room for optimism, for I have cancelled those dismal events years ago.

> *I can no longer afford to give my shame a seat at the head of the table, while my pride quietly serves us.*

My past is just that: my past. Will I still have to contend with being hurt? Yes! However, I refuse to let hurt drain me of my zest for life. I choose to forgive, severing the stranglehold my past once had on me. Today, I no longer view my past as a badge of shame, but I use everything from it as a powerful testimony of deliverance to help others obtain their freedom. With each new revelation of who I am, I become stronger! I consign my past to an instructional role only. From now on, I use it only as a teaching tool to help others sidestep their own foolishness, if they have ears to hear. Otherwise, it no longer has any say in the direction my future will take.

In acknowledging my past, I had to acknowledge my view of the people in it. I realized I could not continue to live my life internalizing everything that happened to me, believing everyone was out to hurt me. There are some things for which I had to take responsibility because I allowed them to happen. Now, I can boldly declare and freely receive into my life the kind of words that are tailor-made specifically for me. I am ready to be fed. This time, I get to choose the meal, the setting, and the desserts.

There was a time I got exactly what I desired, never considering whether it was good for me. I wanted whatever I could get, as long as I got something. It made me feel special. So be mindful when dressing the table. Ensure your settings are from thoughts you manufacture, based on a well-balanced diet. As much as we are forever moving forward, our past is ever present. Therefore, give no place to your past, or you will eventually find yourself back in it.

Although there are things in life we have absolutely no control over, we somehow reach a point in life where we realize we can take control of certain aspects of it by neutralizing the power the past exerts on it. This is cause for great celebration, knowing I do not have to allow my past to control my future. What has happened *to* me does not have to happen *in* me. I can choose to live in the shadow of my past, or I can take life by the reins God gave me and intentionally redirect my future in the direction of my choosing.

I had to decide to no longer live with a "should've, would've, could've" mentality. If things are not different by now, it is only because of me. I acknowledge my past for what it was, and I constantly remind myself it no longer is. I also encourage myself to not live in the past ever again. I now acknowledge and realize I have always had the power to dress the table, and now I am both capable and empowered to do so. Therefore, I gladly come to Sit and Eat.

There is absolutely nothing you may have gone through in life, no matter how pleasant or horrific, that is unique to only you. Your story is your story, but I guarantee you it has been both lived and told before. Could it very well be your voice is the only voice some people are willing to hear? I think it is a fallacy to believe everything happens for a reason, especially when one considers all that happens. But I do believe I can determine how I will allow what has happened to affect me and the rest of my life. I can keep it to myself and watch others die, or I can invite them to my table and help them live.

Released from a table that sheltered dismay, life is now in our hands and WE can make it to our liking. We can, with our own children, create grand memories and feed them words that can guide their lives. They can be invited to a table that harbors no animosity and has released guilt and fear, and share with them a past they will not have to experience. They can go further faster than the journeys we took, because it will never be one they will travel. Prepare your children for life and present them to the world, well done and made to order.

Call Outs and Quotes

Call Outs

Chapter 1
The table becomes a common ground that minimizes all differences while exposing them at the same time.

The table must be preserved as the one place where the official, unwritten rule must be: Listen to me and hear me out.

Chapter 2
I saw the table as a "no judgment zone" where I could expose my deepest fears and insecurities without feeling naked before the world.

Each and every day, the issues of life challenge us to define who we truly are, and there is absolutely no better place to be you than in the company of family and friends, all together in one place—hopefully at the table.

Chapter 3
"Words—so innocent and powerless as they are, as standing in a dictionary, how potent for good and evil they become in the hands of one who knows how to combine them."

When you know that someone will celebrate you with their presence and with their words of encouragement, those gestures have the ability to draw the best out of you.

We have come to understand the value of words to the point where we want to make sure our words are the ones which speak loudest, are most influential, are balanced, and are the truth.

Chapter 4
Most of the words we receive from others are not sturdy enough to support our aspirations; neither are they enriched with the proper nutrients to cause growth in our lives.

The main difference between the service you get at a restaurant and the people you encounter daily is that the restaurant service will be spot-on much of the time, whereas one hundred percent of the people you deal with daily will possess flaws and imperfections.

The quality of the information you take in will be determined largely by the people you allow to speak into your life.

Chapter 5
We have collected the measly crumbs that have fallen from the lips of every childhood friend and every teacher who has ever told us who we were not (or would never become), and we have pounded these crumbs into a form that has become our own self-image.

The more words you hear that are right and life-building, the easier it becomes to weed out the wrong words and the people who deliver them.

Chapter 6
Learn to take every bit of instruction and difficult-to-swallow correction as an opportunity to grow and improve.

Live so we can be inspired by your story!

Chapter 7

We have to decide whether we want to live in the pain of our past or the possibilities of our future, sorting out the pieces as we go.

I can no longer afford to give my shame a seat at the head of the table, while my pride quietly serves us.

Quotes

"A single conversation across the table with a wise man is better than ten years mere study of books."
Henry Wadsworth Longfellow

"Lost time is never found again."
Benjamin Franklin

"We do not remember days; we remember moments."
Cesare Pavese, The Burning Brand

"A picture can tell a thousand words, but a few words can change its story."
Sebastyne Young

"Just because someone talks, does not make them qualified to speak. Just because you hear them, does not mean you have to listen."
Talisha Bennett

"I am not interested in picking up crumbs of compassion thrown from the table of someone who considers himself my master. I want the full menu of rights."
Bishop Desmond Tutu

"Nothing is better for self-esteem than survival."
Martha Gellhorn

"It is your reaction to adversity, not the adversity itself, that determines how your life's story will develop."
Dieter F. Uchtdorf

About the Author

Talisha L. Bennett is the wife of author and music artist, Charles Bennett, and mother of four. She spent the majority of her teen years growing up in New Orleans, LA, while her formative years were spent as a proud daughter of an enlistee of the United States Air Force. Talisha is a veteran of the United States Air Force and an alumnus of the University of Phoenix, from which she holds both a Bachelor of Science in Business with a concentration in Accounting and a Master of Business Administration.

www.ingramcontent.com/pod-product-compliance
Lightning Source LLC
Chambersburg PA
CBHW072101290426
44110CB00014B/1778